# Checkpoint Cisco ASA Firewall and Linux Admin Interview Questions And Answers

## - 3 Books in 1 –

Checkpoint Firewall Admin Interview Questions and Answers

Cisco ASA Firewall Interview Q&A

Interview Guide for Linux Administrator

By

Salsag Gulberg  Mark Tim  Mike Ryan

# Copyright © 2018

**ISBN:** 9798611289235

# License Notes

# Table of Contents

CHECKPOINT
FIREWALL INTERVIEW
QUESTIONS AND ANSWERS
FACE THE INTERVIEW WITH CONFIDENCE
MARK TIM

# Checkpoint Firewall Admin Interview Questions and Answers

*Face the interview with confidence*

By Mark Tim

# Copyright © 2018 Mark Tim

# License Notes

This book is licensed for your personal enjoyment only. This book may not be re-sold or given away to other people. If you would like to share this book with another person, please purchase an additional copy for each recipient. If you're reading this book and did not purchase it, or it was not purchased for your use only, then please return to amazon.com and purchase your own copy. Thank you for respecting the hard work of this author.

# Also, By Mark Tim

Linux Administrator Top Interview Question and Answers

Linux Security Beyond System Administration

Network Admin Top Interview Questions and Answers

Interview Question And Answers For
AWS Developers And Architects

Azure Top Interview Questions and Answers

# Chapter 1:
# Introduction

Checkpoint is one of the leading security software development multinational company that provide various software and hardware products/solutions related to IT security including endpoint security, mobile security, network security, data security and Security Management products. Checkpoint CEO, Gil Shwed pioneered the I.T. security industry with product FireWall-1 and its patented Stateful inspection technology, which is still the foundation for most network security technology today.

For the eighteenth consecutive year, Check Point has been positioned in the "Leaders" quadrant in the Magic Quadrant for Enterprise Network Firewalls

The objective of this document is cover Q&A notes for Admins preparing for Checkpoint interview. It will also try to cover Job responsibility and some common troubleshooting tips.

# Chapter 2:
# Interview Questions and Answers

**• What is Statefull Inspection?**

*Ans*: Statefull inspection is also known as dynamic packet filtering. In this type of inspection, firewall creates connection state information for protocols like TCP, UDP, and ICMP etc. Therefore, if traffic is permitted by Access policies then a connection state is created and reverse traffic (from destination to original source) is allowed.

**• What is the Operating System of Checkpoint Called?**

*Ans*: Checkpoint Operating System is called as GAIA. Previous versions were SPLAT and IPSO

**• What is the latest version of Checkpoint? Or what is the latest version of Checkpoint you are working with?**

*Ans*: As of today, the latest version of Checkpoint is R80.10. Checkpoint recently released it R80 (major version) claiming a gold standard management in firewall management history. But customer are still using R77.X versions

• **What does SMART means in Checkpoint Architecture?**

***Ans***: SMART in Checkpoint means Security Management Architecture. With SMART Security Administrator can centrally, configure, manage and report on all security devices including endpoints, from a single console - **The SmartDashboard**

• **Is Checkpoint a Zone based Firewall?**

***Ans***: No

• **What are the core component of Checkpoint Core technology?**

***Ans***: Checkpoint Core System consists of three core components:

• Smart Console (Also called as GUI Client) SmartConsole is a windows system in which SmartConsole client application is installed. Smart console consists of several clients (like SmartDashboard, Smartview monitor, Smartview Tracker, Smart update etc.) used to manage different checkpoint products

• Security Management Server (SMS) also called as SmartCenter Security Management stores and distribute policies to multiple security gateway from Single management console. SMS maintains all the database like network-objects, users, security policies, and signature database and log files of firewalls.

• Security Gateway: Security Gateway is the firewall machine on which firewall software is installed. Security policies are defined in SmartDashboard and saved in Security management and pushed to firewall as inspection script. Security gateway is just an inspection device

• **Where does Checkpoint inspection script insert itself in OSI layers?**

*Ans*: In between Datalink and Network

• **In what deployment modes, Checkpoint products can be installed?**

*Ans*: Checkpoint products can be installed as below:

**Standalone deployment**: In standalone deployment mode, Security gateway and management server are installed in same computer or hardware

**Distributed Deployment**: In distributed deployment mode, Security gateway and management are installed in different computer or hardware.

**Standalone FULL HA deployment**: In a standalone Full HA deployment mode, the security gateway and management are each installed on one appliance and two appliances working in High Availability mode.

**Bridge mode**: Bridge mode add security gateway to an existing environment without any IP routing changes

• **Which Smartconsole application will be used to add/remove policies, view logs and monitor gateway resources, license and contract info?**

*Ans*:

SmartDashboard  Is used for adding/removing policies, creating/deleting objects,

Smartview Tracker  Is used for viewing logs

Smartview Monitor  Is used for monitoring gateway resources

Smartupdate  view and update License and contract information

## • Which SmartConsole application is used to disconnect GUI Client from SmartConsole applications?

***Ans***: Login to Smartview Monitor application  disconnect client disconnect the user from Smartconsole clients

## • What is Secure Internal Communication (SIC)?

***Ans***: The Security Management Server (SMS) should be able to communicate with all of its components and OPSEC applications through a secure medium even though they are installed on difference machine, this secure channel is called as SIC.

The SIC creates a trusted status between Gateways, Management servers and other Check Point components. SIC is required to install polices on Gateways and to send logs from Gateways to Management servers.

These security measures ensure the security of SIC:

• Certificates for authentication

• Standards-based Secure Sockets Layer (SSL) for the creation of the secure channel

• 3DES for encryption

• **How can we reset SIC?**

***Ans***: From the command line, type cpconfig  Secure Internal Communication  Re-initialize communication


• **What are the software bundles that a customer can buy with Checkpoint security gateway?**

***Ans***:

Next Generation Firewall (NGFW) Statefull Firewall + Application Control + IPS

Next Generation Threat Prevention (NGTP)  Statefull Firewall + IA + Application Control + URL Filtering + IPS + AV/AB + Anti-spam/Email Security

Next Generation Data Loss Prevention (NGDP)  Statefull Firewall + IA + Application Control +  IPS + DLP

Next Generation Threat Extraction (NGTX)  Statefull Firewall + IA + Application Control + URL Filtering + IPS + AV/AB + Anti-spam/Email Security + SandBlast Threat Emulation & SandBlast Threat Extraction


• **Which blades allows access control based on users?**

***Ans***: Identity Awareness and VPN blade

## • What are the two basic rules used by all security administrators?

*Ans*:

Stealth Rule: Stealth rule prevents users from directly connecting to firewall. This will help only authorized users like IT admins/Firewall Admins to have access to Firewall. In most of the cases, stealth rule should be kept on the top of firewall rule base

Cleanup Rule: Security gateway drops all the communications which are not explicitly defined in firewall rule base. Cleanup rule is used to monitor all the dropped packet and are logged. Cleanup rules are placed at the last of firewall rule base

## • Rule order in Checkpoint:-

First rule (Implied rule)

Explicit rules

Before Last rule

Last rule

Implicit Drop rule (at the end)

*If You enjoy this book which you are about to read, would you please consider to leave a review. You can click the below link or visit Amazon product page to write a review.*

*Please visithttps://www.amazon.com/review/create-review?asin=B078TQRQ1Y to write a review.*

## • What is Anti-spoofing?

***Ans***: Anti-spoofing feature in checkpoint firewall verifies packet are coming from and going to, the correct interface. It also confirms that packets coming from internal network are actually coming from true internal network interface.

Anti-spoofing is implemented on a specific interface and spoof tracking for that interface should also be defined.

## • What is Database Revision Control?

***Ans***:

Database revision control takes snapshot of objects, policies, IPS updates etc. It allows administrator to create fallback configurations while implementing new objects, rules or adjusting rules and objects as network change. This will help firewall administrators to test rule base configurations/objects or revert to an earlier state for troubleshooting.

## • What is a policy package?

***Ans***: In some circumstances, we may require multiple version of security policy, yet object database needs to be same. Often this will occur when adding or consolidating rules in an existing Rule Base or when creating a new set of rules on a Gateway. Policy package allows us to create multiple policy sets that can be installed on different gateways. It allows us to group different type of policies to be installed together on same installation targets. It also allows us to associate each policy package to appropriate set of gateways.

• **What connection persistence attributes are present in Checkpoint security gateway?**

*Ans*: There are the three connection persistence option:

Keep all connections: keeps all control and data connections open until the connections have ended. The newly installed policy will be enforced only for new connections

Keep Data Connections: keeps all data connections open until the connections have ended. Control connections that are not allowed under the new policy will be terminated

Rematch Connections: means that all connections not allowed under the new policy will be terminated, unless the service has Keep connections open after policy has been installed is enabled in the Service Properties window

**Default setting for connection persistence is: Rematch connection. It can be checked under gateway/gateway cluster properties other connection persistence**

• **From which command, we can check policy installed on gateway?**

*Ans*: fw stat (It will help to verify which policy package is installed in which gateway)

• **Which command is used to check security gateway version?**

*Ans*: fw ver

**• Which command is used to check checkpoint processes status?**

***Ans***: cpwd_admin list

**• How can you remove all the policies from gateway?**

***Ans***: fw unloadlocal (It will remove all the existing security policies from the gateway, May be helpful during lock out situation)

**• What do you mean by NAT?**

***Ans***: NAT means Network Address Translation. NAT allows administrator to overcome the limitation of public IPs. It enables private IP network that use unregistered IP address to connect to Internet. If, IP address of client initiating a connection is translated then it is called Source NAT (SNAT). If, IP address of machine receiving a connection is translated then it is called Destination NAT (DNAT)

Types of NAT:

Hide NAT: It is a many-to-one relationship where multiple computers on the internal network are represented by a single unique address. This type of NAT is also called as Dynamic NAT.

Static NAT: It is a one-to-one relationship where each host is translated to a unique address; this allows connections to be initiated internally and externally

## Ways of writing NAT policies

**Automatic NAT**: In automatic NAT configuration, Security gateway makes all the necessary route and ARP table entries and is configured under network object NAT tab. Automatic NAT rule is suitable for most standard installations.

**Manual NAT**:  In Manual NAT, NAT rules are created manually. Manual NAT rule creation may be desired in below situation:

• Situations where translation is desired for some services and not for others.

• When port Address Translation is required.

• Environments where more granular control of Address Translation is required

• Where NAT translation order must be manipulated


• **Fwmonitor and tcpdump**

*Ans*:

FWmonitor is a checkpoint's powerful packet capture which captures network packets at multiple capture points along the FireWall inspection chains. Later, these packets can be analyzed using Wireshark. It is supported to run only a single instance of FW Monitor at any given time. To run fwmonitor effectively, it is recommended to disable SecureXL. There are four inspection points when a packet passes through Checkpoint gateway.

• Inbound => Before the inbound FW VM => Pre-Inbound => "i"

• Inbound => After the inbound FW VM => Post-Inbound => "I"

• Outbound => Before the outbound FW VM => Pre-Outbound => "o"

• Outbound => After the outbound FW VM => Post-Outbound => "O"

The traffic direction inbound/outbound refers to each packet not connection

Tcpdump is packet capture utility that runs on command line and is used to capture TCP/IP packets flowing on a network.

<u>Notes on Tcpdump</u>:

CTRL+C Stops tcpdump capture

With –i  switch, tcpdump can be run on specific interface . For e.g. tcpdump –i eth0

With –e  switch, it displays source and destination mac address .

By default, only first 68 bytes of packet is captured, with switch –s , size of packet can be increased.

**• From which tools we can check traffic logs, active logs, and Management/audit logs?**

***Ans***: We can check traffic logs from Smartview Tracker  Network & Endpoint Tab

Active connections on gateway through Smartview Tracker  Active tab

And Audit logs through Smartview Tracker  Management tab

By default, current traffic log is stored in $FWDIR/log/fw.log file

Active connections log are stored in $FWDIR/log/fw.vlog file

Management log are stored in $FWDIR/log/fw.adtlog file

## • Which Management blade will help report generation?

***Ans***: SmartEvent and SmartReporter blade

## • What is SAM Rule?

***Ans***: SAM stands for Suspicious Activity Monitoring. It's a utility that is integrated with SmartView Monitor. Suspicious activity rules are the firewall rules that helps administrator to instantly block suspicious host/connection without the need to perform an Install Policy operation from SmartDashboard.

## Configuring Suspicious Activity Monitoring rule:

• Log in to Smartview Monitor

• Go to Tools & Suspicious Activity rule

• Click Add

• From, Apply On, select specific gateway where you want install SAM rules

• In the Source field, define source host or network/network mask

• In the destination field, define destination host or network mask

• In the service field, define service that you want to block

• In the expiration section, define relative time in which the rule should expire or absolute time in which rule should expire

• In the advanced button, define whether to Drop, Reject or Notify in Action tab and in the Track define whether to log , No log or Alert that connection

• Click Enforce, to apply that rule


• **What is VPN?**

***Ans***:  VPN stands for Virtual Private Network. VPN allows us to extend private network over unsecure public network like internet and share file/resources as if they are on private network.

Types of VPN:

• Site to Site VPN

• Remote Access VPN

Commonly used VPN protocols

• IPsec

• L2TP

• PPTP etc.


• **Explain the License scheme used in Checkpoint**

***Ans***: Checkpoint licensing scheme is very scalable and modular and offers both predefined bundles as well as customer ability to build solution as per their needs. Most of the Checkpoint software on the installation media is automatically enabled for 15 days trial license.

License activation can be done either online or offline. For online activation, appliance should have connectivity to internet and fetch license from Checkpoint website

For offline activation, An administrator needs to download license file from Checkpoint website and needs to add license via Smartupdate.

## Service Contract File:

A service contract file is a file which hold all the information about checkpoint product service contracts. In most of the case, Security management is configured to automatically communicate with usercenter and download most current contract file.

## Managing Licenses:

Central License: Central license allows security administrator allows license for Security gateway/domain management server to be associated with the IP address of Primary management Server. This provide greater flexibility to add or remove licenses. Central license are installed in license repository of Smartupdate and can be easily attached or detached from the destination machine. Central licensing method are usually suitable for distributed installation

Local License: Local license is associated with the IP address of destination machine in which license is being installed. Every time, IP address of machine changes, a new license has to be generated. Local licensing is easy for standalone installation.

*Note: licenses should not be generated with IP addresses that do not appear in SmartUpdate to the right of the referenced object.*

### • What are ways to perform backup in checkpoint?

***Ans***: There are few ways to take backup of Checkpoint system running GAIA OS. Below are the built-in procedure:

• Snapshot Management (& Revert): This creates entire snapshot of device which include Checkpoint product and its configuration and operating system related configurations. Log partition is not included in snapshot, therefore logs are not backed up in snapshot.

• System backup (& System Restore): Generating System backup creates a compressed file that contains Checkpoint product configurations including networking and operating system parameters such as routing & interface configuration but unlike snapshot, it doesn't include operating system binaries and hotfixes.

In R77.30 in Checkpoint hardware or open server, backup file is stored in location "/var/log/CPbackup/backups/"

In R75.40 - R77.20 Checkpoint hardware, backup file is stored in location "/var/log/CPbackup/backups/"

In R75.40 - R77.20 Open Server, backup file is stored in location "/var/CPbackup/backups/"

*Note: With above backup methods, backup should be resorted in same appliance. Snapshot and show configuration can be restored to machine with different version however System backup can be restored on same version.*

Recommended Backup Plan:

• Snapshot  It should be taken after fresh installation, before an upgrade and before a hotfix installation

• System backup  It should be taken monthly/weekly/daily depending upon how frequently we change rulebase/configuration

• Saving configuration from GAIA CLISH:  This allows us to save GAIA OS configuration by running "show configuration" and saving it to notepad file as ready-to-run CLI script.

• Other Configuration backup tools:

Migrate export (& import): Migrate tools allows us to export/import configuration database from checkpoint management servers.

Procedure:

• On the source server, download migrate tools of target version

• Upload it to directory, $FWDIR/bin/upgrade_tools

• Under same directory, run command "./migrate export <migrate_export>.tgz

• On target server, upload the file <migrate_export>.tgz to directory $FWDIR/bin/upgrade_tools and run command "./migrate import <migrate_export>.tgz"

## • What is ClusterXL?

***Ans***: ClusterXL is software based High Availability and Load sharing solution from Checkpoint that distributes network traffic between clusters of redundant Security Gateways.

ClusterXL provides:

• Transparent failover in case hardware/service failovers

- Zero downtime for mission critical application with state synchronization

- Enhanced Throughput

- Transparent upgrades

ClusterXL uses Cluster Control Protocol (CCP) to pass synchronization and other information between cluster members.

<u>ClusterXL modes</u>:

Load Sharing Multicast Mode:  Traffic is sent to both cluster member and cluster will decide which member should process the traffic

Loadsharing Unicast Mode: Traffic is sent to only one member called pivot member and it will decide whether to process traffic itself or sent to other member

New High Availability Mode: Both cluster member will different IP/MAC. Virtual IP is used with active gateway mac address and traffic is ultimately processed by active gateway. GARP is used to update MAC incase of failover.

Legacy High Availability Mode: Both cluster member uses same IP and MAC and Standby gateway remain inactive unless active gateway fails.

- **From which command we can check cluster status?**

*Ans*: cphaprob stat

## • Checking Cluster health status

***Ans***: Some of the below commands may be useful to check cluster health status;

cphaprob stat

cphaprob –ia if

cphaprob –ia list


## • What is Management High Availability?

***Ans***: Security Management server holds several database such as user database, objects database, policy information and signature database. Management server plays very crucial role in checkpoint architecture. If Primary Management server fails or is down the backup server needs to be in place to take over operations.

In Management High availability, there will be active security management server and other will be backup security management server that are ready to take over active management server in case of failure.

Synchronization in Management HA is done either manually or automatic.

Manual Synchronization: It is manually initiated by administrator.

Automatic Synchronization: In automatic synchronization, administrator will allow standby management server to be synchronized active management server at set of interval time. The basis of synchronization schedule is when:

• Policy is installed or policy is saved

## • How can we enable log rotation?

***Ans***: On the management (log server) server  general properties  Logs  Storage

• Create a new log file when size is greater than X MB

• Create a new log file on scheduled time

## • What is CPinfo?

***Ans***:  CPinfo is a Checkpoint utility that collects diagnostics data on a customer's machine at the time of execution. The CPinfo output allows Checkpoint TAC engineers to analyze customer setup, firewall policies, configurations and environment.

## Usage Instruction:

Under the expert mode:

#cpinfo –z –o <CPInfo filename>

#cpinfo –v  to Check CPinfo version

#cpinfo –y all  to check hotfix installed on machine

## • Commands to check Checkpoint product health status

***Ans***:

Under expert mode:

# top  to Check cpu usage status ( press 1 to see cpu usage breakdown per core and q to quit )

\# du –h  to check disk usage status

\# df –h  to check disk free status

\# free –m  to check memory

\# cplic print –x  to check license status

\# cpview  utility to check checkpoint utilization status

**• What will happen if Management server is down and all of sudden Security gateway restarts?**

*Ans*: Security gateway will install locally fetched policies

**• From where we can verify gateway will fetch or install policy from management server?**

*Ans*: Go to gateway general properties  fetch policy  check whether the desired management server is listed or not

**• What is maximum limit for concurrent connections in Checkpoint Security gateway?**

*Ans*: By default, it is set to Automatic adjustment however we can define maximum limit for concurrent connections manually

**• By default, what IPS profile are present in Checkpoint Security gateway implementation?**

*Ans*: By default, IPS comes with two profile: Default IPS profile, Recommended IPS profile

• **Which Blade is used to filter traffic based on Country?**

*Ans*: IPS blade

• **By default, what ThreatPrevention profiles are present in Checkpoint Security gateway implementation?**

*Ans*: By default, Threat prevention blade comes with recommended ThreatPrevention profile.

• **Which command is used to save configuration in CLISH shell?**

*Ans*: save config

• **Which command is used to check hostname?**

*Ans*: show hostname

• **Which command is used to check interface status?**

*Ans*:

Show interfaces or show interface ethX (where X is interface number like eth0)

• **Which command is used to check routes in Checkpoint devices?**

*Ans*: show route

• **Command to add route in checkpoint device?**

*Ans*: set static-route X.X.X.X/24 nexthop gateway address X.X.X.X on

# Chapter 3:
# Additional CLI Commands
# (R77 GAIA CLI COMMANDS)

Commands related to CP

| | |
|---|---|
| cpstop | Stop all Check Point services |
| cpstart | Starts all checkpoint services |
| cprestart | Stops and starts all checkpoint services |
| cpconfig | Allows you to re-configure to checkpoint configuration like licenses/contract, SIC, Administrator etc. |
| cpwd_admin list | List checkpoint processes |
| cplic print | Print all  licensing information |
| cplic print –x | Print all licensing information with signatures( more useful) |
| cpstat fw ( on Security gateway) | Shows policy name, timestamp, interface table with flow statistics |
| cpstat os –f cpu | Shows CPU status |
| cpstat os –f memory | Shows memory status |
| cpstat os –f disk | Show disk usage status |
| cpstat os -f ifconfig | Shows interface configuration tables |
| cpstat os -f routing | Shows routing table |
| cpstat os -f all | Shows statistical information related to Product, Policy and Status information |
| cp_conf sic state | Show SIC status on gateways |
| cpinfo –z –o <filename> | collects diagnostics data on a customer's machine at the time of execution, compresses the file and save it In the required filename |
| cpinfo –y all | Shows all hotfix installed on machine |
| cpvinfo | Check the version info of a particular file |
| ifconfig [-a] | Shows all interfaces and their settings |

Commands related to FW module

| | |
|---|---|
| fw ver [-k] | Shows firewall's version and Build number |
| fw stat | Shows which policy is installed on gateway |
| fwstart –f | Starts VPN-1 & Firewall-1 Module |
| fw ctl iflist | Displays interface list |
| fw ctl arp | Display proxy arp table. Also try "arp –a" command to see arp tables |
| fw ctl chain | Shows in and out chain of CP modules. |
| fw ctl zdebug drop | lists all dropped packets in real-time gives an explanation why the packet is dropped |
| fw ctl multik stat | Displays multi-kernel statistics for each kernel instance, The number of connections currently being handled, The peak number of concurrent connections the instance has handled since its inception |
| fw ctl affinity -s | Sets CoreXL affinities when using multiple processors |
| fw ctl affinity -l | Lists existing CoreXL affinities when using multiple processors |
| fw ctl pstat | General statistics like  Memory, connections, fragments, sync information etc. about Check Point firewall |
| fw fetch <X.X.X.X> | Fetch the policy and install |
| fw fetch localhost | Fetch policy from local host |
| fw lslogs | Shows the fwlog files and their size |
| fw logswitch | Switch the current fw.log file to a new file with name formatted as Year-Month-Day-HHMMSS.log |
| fw monitor | is a powerful built-in tool to simplify the task of capturing network packets at multiple capture points within the firewall chain |
| fw tab -t connections -s | To check the number of concurrent connections (#VALS) and the peak value (#PEAK) |
| fw tab -t fwx_alloc -x | To clear the NAT tables |
| fw ctl get int [global kernel parameter] | Shows the current value of a global kernel parameter |
| **fw ctl set int [global kernel parameter] [value]** | Sets the current value of a global keneral parameter on the fly |
| fwaccel stat | To see the SecureXL status and templates |
| fwaccel stats | Examine the SecureXL statistics |
| fwaccel on | Turn on SecureXL |
| fwaccel off | Turn of SecureXL |
| fw unloadlocal | Clears the local firewall policy |

Commands related to VPN Module

| Command | Description |
| --- | --- |
| vpn ver [-k] | Display the VPN major version number and build number |
| vpn shell | Starts the VPN Shell |
| vpn tux | Launch the TunnelUtil tool which is used to control VPN tunnels |
| vpn crlview | Retrieve the Certificate Revocation List (CRL) from various distribution points |
| vpn crl_zap | Erase all Certificate Revocation Lists (CRLs) from the cache |
| vpn debug on | Turns on high level VPN debugging & Instruct the VPN daemon to write debug messages to the VPN log file: in $FWDIR/log/vpnd.elg. |
| vpn debug off | Turns off all VPN debugging |
| vpn debug ike on | Turns on IKE packet logging to: $FWDIR/log/IKE.elg |
| vpn debug ike off | Turns of IKE logging |
| vpn drv  on/off | Starts/stops the VPN kernel |
| vpn drv stat | Returns the status of the VPN kernel, whether the kernel is on or off |

# Chapter 4:
# Some common troubleshooting steps

**Scenario 1:  Latency issue**

• Check RX and TX counters for problematic interface to verify traffic consumption ( may use monitoring software as well )

• Check whether interface is over congested or not

• Check whether it's a issue with firewall or ISP itself

• Initiate a continuous ping from firewall(or particular host) itself and measure latency ( must have previous baseline of traffic latency )

• Check CPU and RAM utilization of gateway


**Scenario 2: Unable to access particular destination**

• Check smartview tracker by using source/destination filter

• Check NAT settings if the source/destination need/need not to be translated

• Check whether packet is dropped by Cleanup rule or by other ways ( use fw ctl zdebug + drop)

• Take captures at ingress and egress interface

## Scenario 3: Firewall is down

• Check reachability to firewall from admin network

• Console access to firewall

• Check whether if there is any policy in firewall or not ( fw stat )

• Check gateway /var/log/messages

## Scenario 4: NAT issues

• Check NAT configurations

• Check Access rules required for particular source or destinations

• Check whether particular source or destination is being translated or not in Smartview Tracker

• Check Proxy ARP entries

• Check NAT methods

• Additionally, take fw monitor captures

## Scenario 5: GUI Access issues/Management Access issues

• Check whether appropriate credentials are used or not

• Check whether initiating source host is defined in GUI clients or not

• Check Routing/connectivity

• Check whether fwm process is up and running or not?

• Check CPU/RAM usage via cpview

## Scenario 6: Policy Installation Failure

• Check connectivity from Management to gateway

• Check SIC status from Management to gateway

• High CPU/RAM usage

• Duplicates rules or one rule hiding others


## Scenario 7: Cluster XL issues

• Check whether clusterXl is enabled on both cluster member or not

• Check whether parameters like hardware/software versions are identical in cluster members or not

• Check pnotes status on both cluster members

• Check for any error messages in log files in case issues

• Check whether IGMP is enabled or disabled at both checkpoint and switch end

• Check whether more than one cluster are connected to same segment or vlan


## Scenario 8: Identity Awareness issues

• Check whether connection with AD is working or not

• Try fetching AD tree

• Check whether IP based rule is overriding

• Check connectivity between Gateway and AD

• Check whether 4624,4768,4769,4770 events are generated in AD or not

## Scenario 9: Application and URL issues

• Check whether particular application/URL is allowed in application& URL blade or not

• Check whether firewall have constant connectivity to checkpoint cloud or not

• Check DNS IP in gateway

• Check whether Application URL database are up to date or not

• Check if custom URL need to be created for allowing a connection

• For HTTPS inspection, check whether certificate is being imported in Checkpoint

## Scenario 10: IPS issues

• Make sure IPS is enforced so that traffic are check again IPS signature

• Check whether IPS update is scheduled or not

• Make sure, Security have connection to internet and DNS are defined in gateway for updates

• Check whether if traffic is being blocked by IPS or not from Smartview Tracker

• Check relevant signature severity, performance impact, risk associated with it

• Make sure understand the risk associated with disabling or enabling a particular signature

• If a particular connection is being blocked by IPS then adding exception can help

• We can put IPS profile in detect only for troubleshooting purpose

• Check bypass IPS under heavy load settings under gateway general properties

•Check High CPU/Ram usage events that can cause IPS not to work properly

## Scenario 11: VPN issues

• Check VPN phase I and Phase II status through Smartview monitor or vpn tu from CLI

• Check whether VPN parameters are identical in both sides or not

• Make sure you have defined correct encryption domain at both end

• Make sure appropriate rulebase is there

• If ClusterXL load sharing is enabled, make sure we enable sticky decision function

• Reset VPN tunnel and initiate traffic again

• Collect VPN debugs and submit to TAC for further troubelshooting

# Chapter 5: Job responsibilities of Checkpoint Firewall Admin

• Should be able to support Checkpoint gateway/management setup in Checkpoint's hardware or Open servers

• Should be able to setup and support gateway cluster and Management clusters

• Strong knowledge on networking concepts like Routing, Switching, VLAN, NAT, and Firewall polices etc.

• Strong knowledge of general protocols like TCP/IP, HTTP, HTTPS, DNS, SMTP etc.

• Should be able to support task related to Firewall support and Operations from Level 1 to Level 3

• High level expertise on IPS/IDS, Application control, URL filtering, HTTPS inspection, AV/AB blades, IA, Anti-spam/Email etc.

• Knowledge on Management blades like Logging and status, SmartEvent, SmartReporter, Compliance etc.

• Knowledge of VPN technologies like IPsec Site-to-Site VPN, Remote Access VPN, SSL VPNs etc.

• Expert knowledge on Data Loss Prevention Techniques

• Should be able to take packet capture in Checkpoint and analyze in Wireshark

• Should be able to maintain detail documentation relating process, procedure and standards

• Resolve ticket pertaining to general Firewall support and complex firewall issues

• Outstanding Analytical and Problem solving skills

# Chapter 6:
# Tips on Interview Preparation

• Make sure your resume is perfect and highlights the security technology and exposure you have gain so far

• Make sure you know about the hiring company or do some research about the company and know their business

• Make sure you introduce yourself better during introduction question asked by interviewer. Don't wait for your questions, highlight your skills and exposure during introduction questions only

• Make you prepare general HR questions like: Why do you want this job? How can you benefit the company? Why should we hire you? Your biggest strength/weakness. What mistakes did you do in past and what lessons did you learn from there etc.

• Make sure you understand general protocols like TCP/IP, HTTP, HTTPS, SMTP, DNS etc.

• Make sure you understand general networking technologies like routing, switching, vlans, NAT access policies etc.

• Make sure you understand Checkpoint Architecture and deployment modes

• Make sure you understand common firewall policy practices

• Make you know how to check traffic logs, analyze logs & take traffic captures etc.

• Make sure you understand all Checkpoint Gateway blades and Management blades

• Highlight If you have deployed Checkpoint High-end Appliances

• Highlight if you have done hardening in Firewall as per hardening guide

• Highlight if you have done Firewall auditing as per ISO, NIST, SITG standards etc.

# Chapter 7: Conclusion

Thus, above document will help Checkpoint Firewall to prepare well for interview. Try to give at least four to five interviews for best results.

All the best!

*As an author I highly appreciate the feedback I get from my readers. It helps others to make an informed decision before buying my book. If You have enjoyed this book please consider leaving a short review at the following link.*

*Please visit https://www.amazon.com/review/create-review?asin=B078TQRQ1Y to write a review.*

## Recommended Books for Interview Preparation:

CISCO ASA Firewall Interview Q&A By Salsag Gulberg

**Linux Administrator Top Interview Question and Answers By Mark Tim**

Linux Security Beyond System Administration By Mark Tim

**Network Admin Top Interview Questions and Answers By Mark Tim**

Interview Question And Answers For AWS Developers And Architects By Mark Tim

Azure Top Interview Questions and Answers By Mark Tim

**Day to Day tasks and solutions of Network Administrators By Mike Ryan**

AWS Top Interview Questions and Answers By Mike Ryan

Interview Guide for Linux Administrator By Mike Ryan

VMware Administrator Interview Question And Answers By Brian Williams

# Cisco ASA Firewall Interview Q&A

* Face the interview with confidence.
* Helpful for eleventh hour revision.
* Book contains most likely asked questions and answers.
* Easy to understand, precise and to the point.

SALSAG GULBERG

SALSAG GULBERG

# Cisco ASA Firewall Interview Q&A

By Salsag Gulberg

# License Notes

This book is licensed for your personal enjoyment only. This book may not be re-sold or given away to other people. If you would like to share this book with another person, please purchase an additional copy for each recipient. If you're reading this book and did not purchase it, or it was not purchased for your use only, then please purchase your own copy. Thank you for respecting the hard work of this author.

# Legal Notes

# Introduction

This book is written to have an idea of what questions are asked in interview for candidates facing CISCO ASA firewall admin role. Clear and precise answer or explanation is given to the most likely questions usually asked in interviews.

This book is suitable for beginner level and intermediate level candidates looking to prepare for ASA firewall administrator role.

# Chapter 1.
# Firewall definition, technologies and models.

1. What is a firewall?

2. What are the different firewall technologies?

3. What are the models available in Cisco ASA firewall family and which OS version you have worked on?

4. What are next generation firewalls?

5. Any difference between session and a connection?

## 1. What is a firewall?

A firewall is a system that manages access between two or more networks.

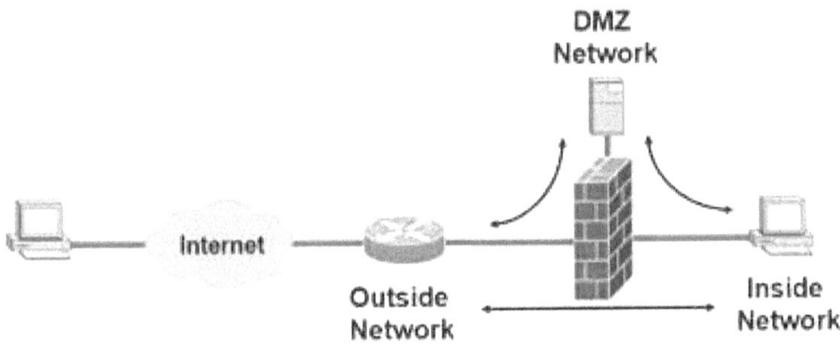


Let's say that in an organization the users in inside network want to access internet, the firewall placed in the network that intercepts the traffic and checks the access. If access is allowed for this particular user to the internet, then access is allowed or else it is denied. The users in the private/LAN network want to access public network then they have to be allowed through the firewall.

Similarly, if the user in the internet that is public network wants to access any of the web servers, application servers or FTP in the DMZ network of organization they have to be allowed through the firewall.

## 2. What are the different firewall technologies?

There are three different firewall technologies:

A. Packet filtering

B. Proxy Server

C. Stateful packet inspection.

A. Packet Filtering: It processes the packets based on the header information. It is based on the access control list technology for providing access. They are much faster but less secure as they work only on layer3 and are not aware of application level attacks.

B. Proxy Server: Proxy servers are usually placed in DMZ zone. It analyses the packets in higher layer of OSI model. Proxy server technology reads all the layer 4 to layer 7 of OSI model and mostly concerned with application layer but are slow in performance.

C. Stateful Packet Inspection: It combines both the functionality of packet filtering and proxy server technology. It maintains complete state data of a session that contains source address, destination address, source port number, destination port number, initial sequence number and flags.

### *State Table in firewall:*

| Source IP | Destination IP | Source port | Destination port | Initial Sequence Number | Ack | Flag |
|---|---|---|---|---|---|---|
| 10.10.1.10 | 172.16.1.9 | 1026 | 80 | 49781 | | syn |
| 192.168.2.20 | 172.16.1.7 | 1026 | 443 | 49576 | | syn |

## 3. What are the models available in Cisco ASA firewall family and which OS version you have worked on?

The models that are available in ASA 5500 series are 5505, 5510, 5520, 5540 and 5580.

The recent models are 5506-X, 5512-X, 5515-X, 5525-X, 55545-X, 5555-X and 5585-X.

The latest software OS version is 9.6(2). The OS version that I have worked on is version 8.2 and 9.1. We can check the latest version of software OS version on www.cisco.com.

You can mention the OS version you have worked on.

## 4. What are next generation firewalls?

Traditional Firewalls performs packet filtering, network and port address translation, stateful inspection and VPN support.

Next generation firewalls: These firewalls apart from doing the tradition firewall functionality they perform deep packet inspection on the payload of the packets and match signatures for harmful activities such as known vulnerabilities, exploit attacks, viruses and malware and integrate with third party such as active directory. It has ability to identify user's identity and enforce policies accordingly.

Thus next generation firewalls do tradition firewalling along with functionalities such as deep packet inspection, intrusion prevention system, website filtering, QOS or bandwidth management, antivirus inspection and identity based policies by integrating with third party such as active directory.

## 5.  Any Difference between a session and a connection?

A connection is communication channel between source and destination PC. After establishing a connection, we can initiate a session. In connection there can be single or multiple sessions.

# Chapter 2.
# Basic commands and features on ASA.

6. Basic Commands on Cisco ASA.

7. What is a security level?

8. What is the difference between transparent mode and routed mode of a firewall?

9. Difference between PIX and ASA.

10. Briefly describe some important features of Cisco ASA firewall?

## 6. Basic commands?

A). Interface

B). nameif

C). ip address

D).Security level

*A). Interface:*

The interface command identifies the hardware interface of firewall.

Following is the command to login to one of the interface g0/0 of a firewall.

ciscoasa (config)#interface g0/0

*B). nameif:*

The nameif command gives the interface a name and assigns a security level.

ciscoasa(config)#nameif outside

INFO: Security level for "outside" set to 0 by default.

*C). ip address:*

This command is used to assign IP address to an interface.

Example: ciscoasa(config)#ip address 192.168.1.1 255.255.0.0

*D). Security-level.*

Security levels are values assigned from 0 to 100 to control the flow of traffic. Example:

ciscoasa(config)#security-level 50.

## 7. What is a Security level?

Security levels in ASA define how much you trust the traffic from that interface. Level 100 is most trusted and level 0 is the least trusted.

Traffic from High to Low it is allowed by default.

For traffic from Low to High we need to allow through ACL between the zones.

Note: Till version 8.2 if nat-control is enable we need to do natting and allow through ACL. And if nat-control is disabled then only ACL needs to be allowed.

After versions 8.2 no need to do natting, we just need ACL to allow communication.

## 8. What is the difference between transparent mode and routed mode of a firewall?

Transparent mode: In transparent mode firewall acts a bump in a wire and both inside and outside interfaces are in the same network.

Routed mode: In routed mode the firewall interfaces are configured in different network.

## 9. Difference between PIX and ASA

A. In PIX AIP SSM module is absent where as in ASA it is present for intrusion prevention.

B. In PIX there is no management port where as in ASA it is present.

C. In PIX we had only two types of licensing, restricted and unrestricted but where as in ASA we have basic, service plus, VPN plus and VPN premium.

## 10. Briefly describe some important features of Cisco ASA firewall?

*A. Proprietary operating system.*

*B. Stateful packet inspection.*

*C. User based authentication.*

*D. Protocol and application inspection.*

*E. Virtual private networking*

*F. Security contexts.*

*G. Web based management.*

# Chapter 3.
# NAT, advantages different types of NAT.

11. What is NAT and its advantages?

12. What are different types of NAT?


## 11. What is NAT and its advantages?

Network address translation (NAT) is designed for IP address conservation. It enables to translate   the private IP address (unregistered IP addresses) to public IP addresses to connect to internet.

### *Advantages of NAT:*

• Enables us to use private IP address and conserve IP address.

• Secures the network from hiding the topology of internal network.

## 12. What are different types of NAT?

*A. Static NAT: Static NAT translations have one to one mapping between private and public IP   addresses. It has two way communications as connection can be initiated from either side.*

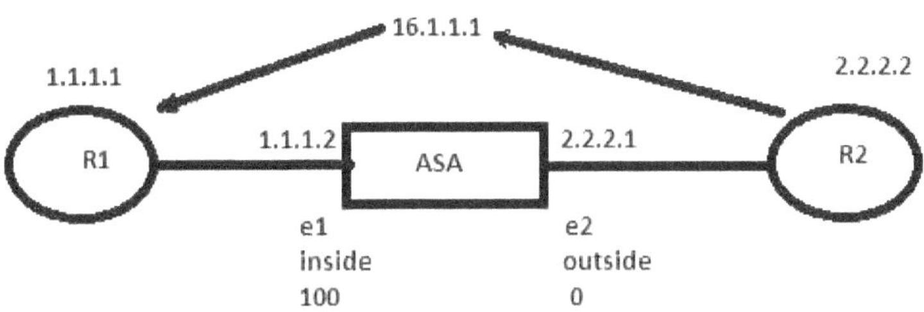



- ASA(config)#object network IN_LANX

- ASA(config)#host 1.1.1.1

- ASA(config)#object network MAPZ

- ASA(config)#host 16.1.1.1

- ASA(config)#nat(inside, outside) source static IN_LANX MAPZ

- ASA(config)#access-list 101 permit ip host 2.2.2.2 host 1.1.1.1

- ASA(config)#access-group 101 in interface outside

## B. Dynamic NAT: In Dynamic NAT translations a pool of private IP addresses are mapped to a pool of public IP addresses. I has one way communication.

- ASA(config)#object network IN_LANX

- ASA(config)#subnet 1.0.0.0 255.0.0.0

- ASA(config)#object network MAP-X

- ASA(config)#range 18.1.1.1 18.1.1.10

- ASA(config)#nat(inside,outside) source dynamic IN_LANX MAPX

- ASA(config)#access-list 102 permit ip IN_LANX any

- ASA(config)#access-group 102 in interface inside


In this example we can see that inside network 1.0.0.0/8 is mapped to range 18.1.1.1 to 18.1.1.10.

We can check using the command #show xlate


**C. NAT Overloading (PAT): In NAT overloading a pool of IP address are mapped to one or more or interface IP address along with the port. It is also called as dynamic PAT.**

It is used to translate the private addresses to one or more public (registered) IP address to access internet.

Unique source port numbers are used to distinguish between the translations during conversation.

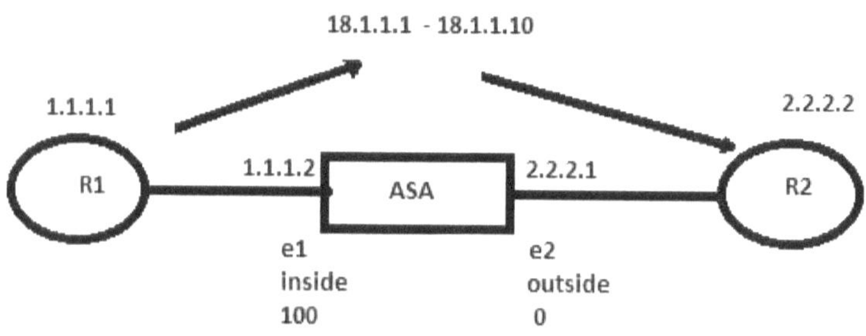

- ASA(config)#object network IN_LANX

- ASA(config)#subnet 1.0.0.0 255.0.0.0

- ASA(config)#object network MAP-X

- ASA(config)#host 17.1.1.1

- ASA(config)#nat(inside,outside) source dynamic IN_LANX
MAPX

- ASA(config)#access-list 102 permit ip IN_LANX any

- ASA(config)#access-group 102 in interface inside

In this example we see that inside LAN 1.0.0.0/8 is mapped to 17.1.1.1 when the traffic is going outside.

Note: One interface only one access-group is allowed.

# Chapter 4.
# .VPN (Virtual Private Network)



## 13. What is a VPN?

Virtual Private Network (VPN): A virtual point to point connection in which encrypted data transfer takes places in secure manner between the two networks is called VPN.

It is like establishing a secure tunnel with encryption, authentication, access control and auditing services over an insecure private or public network without the expense of lease line.

## 14. Why do we need VPN?

We usually establish VPN to

**A. Security.**

**B. Alternative to costly lease lines.**

*A. Security:*

1. Data Confidentiality: It is achieved by encryption of data using encryption algorithms
such as DES, 3DES and AES.

2. Data Integrity: It is achieved by using hashing algorithms such as MD5, SHA and HMAC.

3. Data Authentication: RSA, CA and pre-shared keys.

*B. Alternate to costly lease lines. VPNs are established using internet and dedicated lease lines can be avoided saving huge cost.*

## 15.What is IPsec?

Internet protocol security (IPsec) is protocol suite standard developed by IETF (Internet Engineering Task Force) to for securing Internet Protocol (IP) communication by authenticating and encrypting each packet in communication session.

The IPsec provides cryptographic security services such as authentication, integrity, access control, and confidentiality.

There are two protocols provided by IPSec, they are AH (Authentication Header, protocol number 51) and ESP (Encapsulated Security Payload, protocol number 50).

## 16. What is a Site to Site VPN?

Site to Site VPN is a type of VPN between two LAN. This is usually used when we want to connect to two or more networks or LANS within same office at different locations. It is also used to connect between different organizations according to requirements.

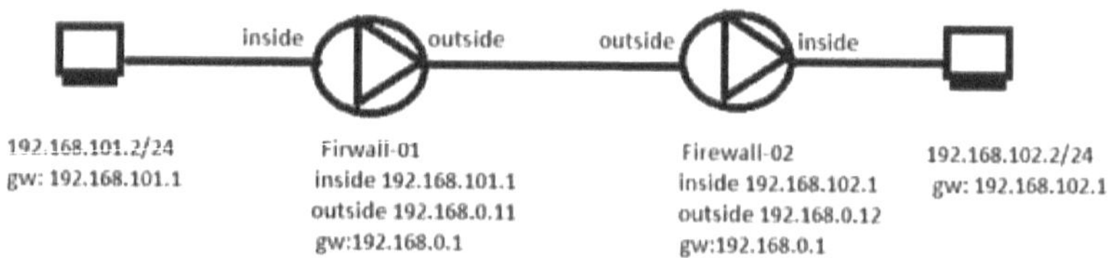


Following is the CLI configuration for site to site VPN. Please consider ASA01 as first firewall and ASA02 as second firewall.

*Configurations*

## <u>ASA01 side configuration:</u>

object network net-local

subnet 192.168.101.0 255.255.255.0

object network net-remote

subnet 192.168.102.0 255.255.255.0

access-list outside_1_cryptomap permit ip 192.168.101.0 255.255.255.0 192.168.102.0 255.255.255.0

tunnel-group 192.168.0.12 type ipsec-l2l

tunnel-group 192.168.0.12 ipsec-attributes

pre-shared-key pass1234

isakmp keepalive threshold 10 retry 2

crypto isakmp enable outside

crypto isakmp policy 10 authentication pre-share

crypto isakmp policy 10 encrypt 3des

crypto isakmp policy 10 hash sha

crypto isakmp policy 10 group 2

crypto isakmp policy 10 lifetime 86400

crypto ipsec transform-set ESP-3DES-SHA esp-3des esp-sha-hmac

crypto map outside_map 1 match address outside_1_cryptomap

crypto map outside_map 1 set pfs group1

crypto map outside_map 1 set peer 192.168.0.12

crypto map outside_map 1 set transform-set ESP-3DES-SHA

crypto map outside_map interface outside

nat (inside,outside) 1 source static net-local net-local destination static net-remote net-remote

route outside 0 0 192.168.0.1


## ASA02  side configuration:

object network net-local

subnet 192.168.102.0 255.255.255.0

object network net-remote

subnet 192.168.101.0 255.255.255.0

access-list outside_1_cryptomap permit ip 192.168.102.0 255.255.255.0 192.168.101.0 255.255.255.0

tunnel-group 192.168.0.11 type ipsec-l2l

tunnel-group 192.168.0.11 ipsec-attributes

pre-shared-key pass1234

isakmp keepalive threshold 10 retry 2

crypto isakmp enable outside

crypto isakmp policy 10 authentication pre-share

crypto isakmp policy 10 encrypt 3des

crypto isakmp policy 10 hash sha

crypto isakmp policy 10 group 2

crypto isakmp policy 10 lifetime 86400

crypto ipsec transform-set ESP-3DES-SHA esp-3des esp-sha-hmac

crypto map outside_map 1 match address outside_1_cryptomap

crypto map outside_map 1 set pfs group1

crypto map outside_map 1 set peer 192.168.0.11

crypto map outside_map 1 set transform-set ESP-3DES-SHA

crypto map outside_map interface outside

nat (inside,outside) 1 source static net-local net-local destination static net-remote net-remote

route outside 0 0 192.168.0.1

For troubleshooting we can use following commands

Phase1: #show crypt isakmp sa   and   Phase2: #show crypto ipsec sa

## 17. What is Client to Site VPN?

Client to site is a type of VPN in which the mobile client can access the inside LAN through internet.

*The following example shows how to configure a remote access IPsec/IKEv2:*

hostname(config)# interface ethernet0

hostname(config-if)# ip address 10.10.4.200 255.255.0.0

hostname(config-if)# nameif outside

hostname(config-if)# no shutdown

hostname(config)# crypto ikev2 policy 1

hostname(config-ikev2-policy)# group 2

hostname(config-ikev2-policy)# integrity sha

hostname(config-ikev2-policy)# lifetime 43200

hostname(config-ikev2-policy)# prf sha

hostname(config)# crypto ikev2 outside

hostname(config)# ip local pool testpool 192.168.0.10-192.168.0.15

hostname(config)# username testuser password 12345678

hostname(config)# crypto ipsec ikev2 ipsec-proposal FirstSet

hostname(config-ipsec-proposal)# protocol esp encryption 3des aes

hostname(config)# tunnel-group testgroup type remote-access

hostname(config)# tunnel-group testgroup general-attributes

hostname(config-general)# address-pool testpool

hostname(config)# tunnel-group testgroup webvpn-attributes

hostname(config-webvpn)# authentication aaa certificate

hostname(config)# crypto dynamic-map dyn1 1 set ikev2 ipsec-proposal FirstSet

hostname(config)# crypto dynamic-map dyn1 1 set reverse-route

hostname(config)# crypto map mymap 1 ipsec-isakmp dynamic dyn1

hostname(config)# crypto map mymap interface outside

hostname(config)# write memory

## 18. What is PFS in VPN?

Perfect Forward Secrecy (PFS) ensures that same key is not generated again during Diffie- Hellman key exchange while establishing VPN.

## 19. What is NAT-Traversal?

NAT-traversal encapsulates IPsec traffic in UDP datagrams using port 4500 thereby providing NAT devices with port information. It is used when the external interface of our firewall is connected to a device that has NAT enabled.

# Chapter 5.
# Router, firewall and IPS

20. What is IPS?

21. Difference between firewall and IPS?

22. Difference between firewall and router?

## 20. What is IPS?

Intrusion prevention System (IPS): It is a system that resides inline the packet stream, blocks the malicious packets and informs the admin.

## 21. Difference between firewall and IPS? Or what firewall can do that IPS cannot?

Firewall manages access between two or more networks whereas IPS blocks the malicious activity and attacks to the network.

Firewall can do the natting that is translating the source IP addresses to public IP address to access internet from local LAN where as an IPS cannot do natting. This is the important feature for which a firewall cannot be replaced by IPS.

## 22. Difference between firewall and a router?

A firewall screens the data that passes through it whereas a router transports the data to right direction between networks.

A router works on layer 3 where as a firewall works from layer 3 to Layer 7. Sometimes firewall works on Layer 2 to Layer7 when configured in transparent mode.

# Chapter 6.
# Day to Day activities, troubleshooting, tools, logging and backup.

23. Packet capture in ASA?

24. How do you enable logging in ASA?

25. How do you take backups?

26. How do you enable ICMP?

27. How do you enable ASDM on firewall?

28. How do you check licensing in appliance?

29. Important TCP/UDP ports used

30. How do you Inspect SMTP/ESMTP traffic in ASA?

31. What are the day to day activities you carry out as a firewall administrator?

## 23.  Packet capture in ASA

Packet capture is a tool in ASA used to capture the incoming packet on the interface for troubleshooting the connectivity problems, monitor suspicious activity, packet sniffing and network fault isolation. We use capture command in ASA to do packet capturing.

*Step1. Configure the access-lists <access-list_name> for capturing the packets that travel from the inside network to the outside network.*

#access-list <access-list_name> extended permit ip host <source_IP_address> host <destination_IP_address>

*Step2. Start the packet capture process using the capture command.*

#capture <capture_name> interface <interface_name> access-list <access-list_name>.

Example: If you want to capture traffic from a source ip 10.254.6.1 to destination IP 172.16.1.10. Then we have to apply the following commands in CLI.

#access-list cap_acl extended permit ip host 10.254.6.1 host 172.16.1.10

#capture capin interface inside access-list cap_acl

Then to view the capture on ASA use the following command:

#show capture capin

#show capture capin detail

*In order to stop the capture at any time, apply the following.*

#no capture command <capture-name>

 Example:  #no capture capin

To clear the capture buffer, apply the following.

# clear capture <capture-name> command

Example: # clear capture capin

## 24. How do you enable logging in ASA

*Logging in ASA is enabled as follows through CLI.*

#logging enable

#logging buffered notifications

#logging trap 3

#logging asdm notifications

#logging host inside <Log_server_IP_address>

## 25. How do you take backups?

Following steps are followed take back from ASA through CLI.

*Step 1. Enable configuration to copy from ASA to TFTP server.*

#tftp-*server interface hostname*

*Step 2. Copy the configuration using copy command as follows:*

#copy startup-config tftp

### *Example:*

#copy startup-config tftp

Address or name of remote host []? *192.168.254.230*

Destination filename [startup-config]? *072407*

!!!!!!

8509 bytes copied in 0.40 secs

Note: You can configure a backup schedule if you want to backup device configurations on a          regular basis. Use 'Device->Configure Backups…' menu command to configure backup schedule.

## 26. How do you enable icmp on firewall?

To allow Icmp we need to configure the firewall to inspect the icmp packets as follows.

ciscoasa(config)#policy-map global_policy

ciscoasa(config-pmap)# class inspection_default

ciscoasa(config-pmap-c)#inspect icmp

## 27. How do you enable ASDM on firewall?

*Following steps are followed to enable ASDM in firewall.*

Firewall_5510#config t

Firewall_5510(config) # enable password xxxxx(your password)

Enable password is necessary to enable ssh access

Firewall_5510(config)# username test password test123

User name and password for connecting using ssh

Firewall_5510(config)# aaa authentication ssh console LOCAL

Different authentication can be configured, like RADIUS, TATAC, etc.., here we specified Local authentication with user name and password mentioned above

Firewall_5510(config)# ssh 10.254.33.215 255.255.255.0 inside

Permit  ssh access to firewall  from specified ip or subnet, inside

Firewall_5510(config)# domain-name asalab.com

Domain name of your company. RSA key is generated using domain name + firewall name combination

Firewall_5510(config)# crypto key generate rsa modulus 1024

Generate RSA key

You are done !!!!!!!!!!!!!!!!!!!!!

Firewall_5510(config)# http server enable

Firewall_5510(config)# http 10.254.33.0 255.255.255.0 inside.

Now we can go to browser and login using https://<IP_address> and install the ASDM software to get dashboard interface.

## 28. How do you check licensing it in appliance?

*We can check license information using following commands:*

# show version

And  # show activation-key

To add activation key to appliance apply the following command.

ciscoasa(config)# activation-key key

ciscoasa(config)# activation-key 0xe02888da 0x4ba7bed6 0xf1c123ae 0xffd8624e

Note: The activation key is not stored in your configuration file. The key is tied to the serial   number of the security appliance. You must reboot the adaptive security appliance after entering the new activation key for the change to take effect in the running image.

## 29.  Important **TCP/UDP** ports used.

*Sometimes port numbers that we usually use in day to day scenarios are asked. Following are some of the port numbers used in day to day operations or defining the rules or ACLs.*

a) FTP – TCP-21

b) SSH – TCP-22

c) Telnet – TCP-23

d) SMTP -  TCP-25

e) DNS – TCP-53 and UDP-53

f) Http – TCP-80

g) Kerberos – TCP-88

h) Pop3 – TCP-110

i) NTP – UDP-123

j) *NETBIOS Name Service- UDP-137*

*k) NETBIOS Session Service Network - UDP-137*

l) SNMP- TCP-161

m) HTTPS – TCP -443

n) System Log listener – TCP-514

o) Print spooler – TCP-515

p) Remote Desktop protocol (RDP) – TCP-3389

q) Sqlnet: TCP-1521

## 30. How do you Inspect SMTP/ESMTP traffic in ASA?

*By default SMTP traffic is blocked to mitigate attacks. We have to enable as follows:*

#class-map inspection_default

#policy-map global_policy

#class inspection_default

#no inspect esmtp

## 31. What are the day to day activities you carry out as a firewall administrator?

*Following are some of the most common day to day activities or responsibilities of a firewall administrator.*

• Manage firewall administration by defining the firewall rules/ ACL in firewall rule base using the source IP address, destination IP address and port number.

• Allow access from local LAN to DMZ / outside network or URLs on internet as per request.

• Regular backups of firewall configuration and whenever major change is scheduled.

• Configure and troubleshoot site to site and client to site VPNs.

• Review logs periodically.

• Take care of inventory of all hardware/software firewalls and OS and coordinate with vendor in case of any hardware failure.

• Troubleshoot network connectivity /internet connectivity issues in day to day operations.

# Conclusion

This book covers most likely asked question in interview while you are seeking for   cisco ASA firewall administrator role in an organization. Each interview will be different and unique but still in all the interviews there are some common questions asked to test the knowledge over the subject. This book address some common questions asked and helps the candidates to prepare and anticipate what kind of questions are asked.

All the best!

# Can I Ask a Favour?

If you enjoyed this book, found it useful or otherwise then I'd really appreciate it if you would post a short review and how it benefited you. I would like read the reviews personally so that I can continually write what people are wanting and serve better.

Thanks for your support!

# INTERVIEW GUIDE

## FOR

# LINUX
# ADMINISTRATOR

1. FACE THE INTERVIEW WITH CONFIDENCE
2. HELPFUL FOR ELEVENTH HOUR REVISION
3. CONTAINS INTERVIEW QUESTIONS AND ANSWERS
4. JOB RESPONSIBILITIES AND TROUBLESHOOTING STEPS
5. EASY TO UNDERSTAND, PRECISE AND TO THE POINT

## MIKE RYAN

# Interview Guide for Linux Administrator

By Mike Ryan

# Copyright © 2018 by Mike Ryan

# License Notes

This book is licensed for your personal enjoyment only. This book may not be re-sold or given away to other people. If you would like to share this book with another person, please purchase an additional copy for each recipient. If you're reading this book and did not purchase it, or it was not purchased for your use only, then please return to amazon.com and purchase your own copy. Thank you for respecting the hard work of this author.

# Also, By Mike Ryan:

AWS Top Interview Questions and Answers

Day to Day tasks and solutions of Network Administrators

# Chapter 1:
# Introduction

This book will enlighten all the beginners, junior and experienced Linux administrators who are willing to tighten their grip over day to day tasks and troubleshoot problems that occurs parallel to that. This book also attempt to prepare you for the job title "Linux Administrator", and should be able to equip you with enough knowledge to go out and be successful in the interview.

# Chapter 2:
# Interview Question and Answers

**Q1. How to exit vi or vim editor?**

**Ans.** Vi has two modes, one for passing functional commands and the other one to edit the content of the file. In order to toggle between these modes we have to press the 'Esc' or escape key. Once we are in the functional mode we can type :q to quit the vi editor without making any further changes, :q! to quit and undo any changes made while type :wq to write the changes and then quit. For example:

*:q*

*:q!*

*:wq*

**Q2. What's the purpose of LVM?**

**Ans.** Logical Volume Manager (in short LVM) is used to serve the purpose of creating/resizing/deleting of a logical volumes (i.e. virtual partitions) on Linux file system. These logical volumes changes are effected immediately to the running operating system without the need of rebooting the OS.

## Q3. Explain the purpose of sar command?

**Ans.** System Activity Report (in short **sar**) is used to serve the purpose of collecting, reporting and saving the Memory, CPU and I/O usage. It generates reports in real-time and can be used to save them as log files.

*/home/fred/ 10.0.0.2((rw)*

## Q4. How can you create partitions in a raw disk?

**Ans. fdisk** utility can be used to create new partitions on the raw disk. Following steps can go through you doing this task:

• ***fdisk /dev/hd**** (for IDE hard disks) and ***/dev/sd**** (for SATA)

• Then type 'n' in order to create the new partition

• In order to make the changes permanent to partition table we will have to write them by pressing 'w' key and hit enter.

## Q5. What is the location for kernel modules?

**Ans.** We can use **lsmod** command to see the list of all installed Linux kernel modules, while all the compiled drivers and kernel modules are stored at ***/lib/modules/(kernel version)*** directory.

## Q6. Define umask.

**Ans.** In Linux whenever a file is created it is predefined by a default set of permissions. User file creation mask (in short **umask**) is the command which determines this default permission mask for any new file to be created. There's a series of octal codes that represents how the permissions are going to take effect. From 0 to 7 each code indicates a different permission mask with 0 meaning anything can be set to 7 means all permissions are prohibited. These can be in 4 digits total (i.e. 0022) first belongs to special permissions section (i.e. setuid, setgid, or sticky) second for user/owner, 3rd for group and 4th for others. For example 0022 **umask** means user/owner can be set as any permission but for group and others write permission is disabled by default.

## Q7. Can you set *umask* permanently for the users? If yes how?

**Ans.** Yes we can set a permanent **umask** for a user, we can achieve this by setting it in the appropriate profile of that user which its shell depends on.

## Q8. How do you change the run level for Linux permanently?

**Ans.** The default run level setting can be found at */etc/inittab* file and we can change the numeric value which corresponds to the run level number (i.e. **id:3:initdefault:**). Any changes to this file will have permanent effect.

## Q9. How do you change the run level for Linux temporarily?

**Ans. init** command can be used to change the run level temporarily. It can either be changed again by typing same command or the run level will be changed back to its default setting once system is rebooted. (E.g. init 5 to go to desktop mode).

## Q10. How does directory sharing works with NFS?

**Ans.** Any directory can be shared using '*/etc/exportfs*' by adding share path, ip and sharing options: For example

*/home/fred/ 10.0.0.2((rw)*

## Q11. What is the method to check NFS shares and how to mount one?

**Ans. showmount** command can display the list of directories that are shared on NFS while 'mount' command additional option of NFS can mount a directory over NFS. For example:

*user@server:/# mount –F nfs remote:/directory /local-directory*

## Q12. What are the default ports for following services: FTP, SSH, SMTP,DNS,DHCP,Squid and MySQL?

**Ans.** FTP runs on 21, SSH on 22, SMTP on 25, DNS on 53, DHCP on UDP 68/69, Squid on 3128, and MySQL on 3306

## Q13. How will you define Network Bonding?

**Ans.** Network bonding is a technique in which more than one Network Interface are bond together for the purpose of redundancy (primarily) and eventually for increased throughput as well. It is also known as Network Interface Card (NIC) Teaming.

## Q14. How many types of Network bonding modes are there?

**Ans.** There are 7 types of network bonding modes:

**(Balance-rr) Mode 0** is default mode and it supports Round-robin policy. Its primary role is to provide fault tolerance and load balancing.

**(active-backup) mode 1** follows the Active-backup policy to provide fault tolerance to network bond.

**(balance-xor) mode 2** is based on exclusive-or (in short XOR) policy.

**(Broadcast) mode 3** follows the broadcast policy to transmit all the data to all the slave interfaces.

**(IEEE 802.3ad) mode 4** based on IEEE 802.3ad standards that uses Dynamic Link Aggregation mode.

**(balance-tlb) mode 5** based on Transmit Load Balancing (in short TLB) mode to provide load balancing and fault tolerance.

**(balance-alb) mode 6** based on Active Load Balancing (in short ALB) mode to provide load balancing and fault tolerance.

## Q15. What's the commands for checking and verifying status of bond interface?

**Ans.** We can check the status of all the shared NFS folders by using the cat command along with the path of the file which contains the content of NFS folders details. For example

*user@server:/ #   cat /proc/ net/ bonding/ bond(n)*

Where (n) is the number of bond (i.e. bond0, bond1, bond2, etc.)

## Q16. What command are used to check the default routing table?

**Ans.** routing table be checked using two commands, traditionally with

*user@server:/# route -n*

and other one is

*user@server:/# netstat -nr*

## Q17. How to look for which ports are open and listening?

**Ans.** We can use two commands to check for open ports on a Linux system. One of them is a traditional command using

*user@server:/# netstat -listen*

while the other one is

*user@server:/# lsof -i*

## Q18. How to list all the services running at a particular run level?

**Ans.** The chkconfig -list command will list all the services running on all run levels but if you want to check for a particular run level's running service then the usage of grep will come handy. For example

*user@server:/# chkconfig –list | grep 3:on*

Will selectively display services running at run level 3 only.

## Q19. How do you enable a service at just a particular run level?

**Ans.** In order to enable a service on particular run level we will use chkconfig command. For example:

*user@server:/# chkconfig <name of service> on –level 5*

## Q20. What command is used to upgrade Linux kernel?

**Ans.** It is not recommended to directly upgrade the kernel as it can cause trouble rebooting the system back. Alternate solution is to install the latest version of kernel using rpm (or native package manager of your Linux distro).

## Q21. How will you look for WWN numbers of HBA cards?

**Ans.** systool command with fc_host option and combined with grep is used to display the WWN numbers of HBA cards. For example:

*user@server:/# systool –c fc_host –v | grep port_name*

## Q22. What's the method to add or change the kernel parameters?

**Ans.** permanent changes to kernel parameters are achieved by first editing the ***/etc/sysctl.conf*** file and then in order to commit the changes permanently we will need to type

*user@server:/# sysctl -p*

## Q23. Define a Puppet Server?

**Ans.** Puppet is based to run on multiple Unix-like Operating system including Linux. Its push configuration type of software that push config to its clients (also known as puppet agents) using its own kind of declarative code. It is used to perform operations like installing a software, checking for the file permissions or updating details on a user account and plenty of other tasks.

## Q24. What is the purpose of manifests in a Puppet server?

**Ans.** The purpose of Manifests files in Puppet server is to provide configuration specifications.

## Q25. What path does puppet master stores its certificate files?

**Ans.** The certificate files for puppet master are at location

*user@server:/ #   /var/ lib/ puppet/ ssl/ ca/ signed*

*If You enjoy this book which you are about to read, would you please consider to leave a review. You can click the below link or vIsIt Amazon product page to write a review.*

*Please visit https://www.amazon.com/review/create-review?asin=B0793LSXXS to write a review.*

## Q26. How do you find only the regular files in a directory?

**Ans.** By using the command **'find'** with flag **-type f** we can search for regular files in a directory. Examples are:

*user@server:/# find /home/fred/ -type f*

*user@server:/# find /var/www/ -type f*

*user@server:/# find / -type f*

## Q27. What is most convenient way of checking for total size of a directory and its subdirectories?

**Ans.** One of the convenient way is to use du command with –sh flag (so we can get total size in much easier format) for example:

*user@server:/# du -sh*

## Q28. How to change 'file permissions only' of all the files from current and subdirectories without changing the directory permissions?

**Ans.** Following command can achieve this:

*user@server:/# find . -type f -exec chmod 644 {} +*

Where '.' represents the current path and '**-type f**' means files only.

## Q29. How to change the 'directory permissions only' of all the files from current and its subdirectories without changing the files permissions?

**Ans.** Following command can achieve this:

*user@server:/# find . -type d -exec chmod 755 {} +*

Where '.' represents the current path and '**-type d**' means directories only.


## Q30. How to show customized columns through 'ps' command?

**Ans.** There are plenty of columns which can be displayed through 'ps' command. It depends on what we are looking for and accordingly we can following potential columns:

| Column Header | Contents |
| --- | --- |
| %CPU | Display CPU usage |
| %MEM | Display memory usage |
| ADDR | Display of the Memory address of the running process |
| C or CP | Display CPU usage alongside the scheduling information |
| COMMAND | Full name of the running process, with arguments (if any) |
| NI | Display nice value |
| F | Display Flags |
| PID | Display Process ID number |
| PPID | Displays parent process's ID number |
| PRI | Display Priority of the process |

| Column Header | Contents |
| --- | --- |
| RSS | Display Real memory usage |
| S or STAT | Display Process status code |
| START or STIME | Display the time when the process was started |
| SZ | Display the usage of Virtual memory |
| TIME | Display the total CPU usage (since uptime) |
| TT or TTY | Display the terminal associated with the process |
| UID or USER | Display process owner's username |
| WCHAN | Display memory address of the event the process is waiting for |

*For example:*

*user@server:/# ps -o user,pid,time,cmd*

## Q31. How do you check which distribution and version of Linux you are using?

**Ans.** Every major distribution (and distros based on them) have a release file stored at /etc/ path. They contain the information regarding the distribution's name, version and more. We can use cat command to print the content of that file:

*user@server:/# cat /etc/*-release*

Here, a wildcard is used prior to –release because different flavours use different name so it's better to use a wildcard (i.e /etc/redhat-release)

## Q32. How do you see which USB and PCI devices are installed on your system?

**Ans.** **lspci −tv** is used to display PCI installed devices, while **lsusb − tv** is used to display USB devices on a Linux system.

## Q33. While *top* command display top running process, which command provides interactivity to this?

**Ans.** We can use **htop** command for interactivity with top running process in Linux, however it may not be available in some installations and you may have to installed it using yum , apt-get (or native package manager)

## Q34. If there's an error at a specific line of a readable file (i.e. config file) how would you nano yourself to that exact line directly?

**Ans.** A flag +n would be used against **nano**. For example:

*user@server:/#  nano +13 file.conf*

## Q35. Most of the big servers have huge log files. How do you check the most recent lines from the logs?

**Ans.** We can use **tail** command to approach this concept. Following is the example of displaying last 50 lines from the log:

*user@server:/#  tail 50 /var/log/messages*

## Q36. How do you get to know which files were executed by which user?

**Ans. lsof –u (username)** will display all the files executed by the given username.

## Q37. How would you run a program as a background process?

**Ans.** By simply putting the & in front of any application will make it run as a background process. For example:

*user@server:/# openvpn &*

## Q38. How do you view and configure network drivers and hardware settings of a network interface?

**Ans. ethtool** is a handy tool for such purpose. It can be used as follow:

*user@server:/# ethtool eth1*

From above example **ethtool** will display information about network interface **eth1**

## Q39. Can you do a "whois" search on a domain from within Linux? If yes how?

**Ans.** Doing a "whois" search on a domain is as easy as it sounds. Just type **whois** and domain name:

*user@server:/# whois google.com*

## Q40. How do you get to know which program is running on what port number?

**Ans.** A simple command of **netstat** with useful flags can achieve this:

*user@server:/# netstat -nutlp*



## Q41. How do you find a file larger than and smaller than specified file size?

**Ans.** The **find** command can be used with its available options to achieve this task:

*user@server:/# find /home -size +70M*

Look for files exceeding 70 MB under /home and its subdirectories

*user@server:/# find /home -size -70M*

Look for files less than 70 MB under /home and its subdirectories



## Q42. What is fail2ban?

**Ans.** Fail2ban is part of intrusion prevention system as it aim to protect password authentication of the server and services running on it from brute force attacks.



## Q43. How do you enable fail2ban for Apache (http(s)) authentication?

**Ans.** Within the configuration file of fail2ban we will have to look for the section by the name [apache] and enable it by settings its value to "true" (if it's not already this way).

*user@server:/ # nano /etc/fail2ban/jail.conf*

*[apache]*

*Enable = true*

## Q44. What's the difference between rsync and scp ?

**Ans.** Secure Copy (in short **scp**) uses straight forward method to copy files from source to destination using ssh as communication medium. Whereas **rsync** uses somewhat algorithms to ensure checksum while file transfer.

## Q45. What are two major types of boot loaders and what is the difference between them?

**Ans.** GRUB and LiLo are the two major types of Linux boot loaders. GRUB is much enhanced boot loader compared to LiLo as it supports better CLI interface, interactive configuration and boot from network support.

## Q46. How do you make a tape archive file of a directory and send it to /dev/tape?

**Ans.** we use tar command to create a tape archive file out of a director. For example:

*user@server:/ # tar -cvf /dev/tape /fred*

## Q47. What are snapshots in Virtual Server environments?

**Ans.** Snapshots are a form of a backup of your machine. They are the type of backup that can be saved as an image and when restored your system will be working exactly in same environment and configuration. Snapshot not only backup your files but also the 'State' of the operating system so it is one of the most reliable form of backups.

## Q48. What is the difference between Anacron and Cron?

**Ans.** Following is a brief comparison of both:

• Cron can be set to run a job for as quickly as after each minute whereas Anacron can run a job in a day not minutes.

• Cron jobs can be setup by any normal user on the machine whereas Anacron can only be set by the super user on the system.

• Cron jobs are skipped if the system is down and schedule has passed. While Anacron job will be execute upon whenever the system is up and running.

• Cron is best for servers and works smooth with desktops and laptops as well, while Anacron is mostly deal for laptops and desktops only.

• Cron jobs are time sensitive, they adhere strictly to minute and hour's calculation while Anacron does not work based on hour or minute calculation.

## Q49. What is IP Masquerade function in Linux?

**Ans.** IP Masquerade in a Linux environment is a networking function which works similar to Network Address Translation (NAT). It helps all other internally connected LAN nodes to reach to the external network (i.e. Internet) through the system on which Masquerade has been enabled and configured.

## Q50. How do you enable IP Masquerading on Linux?

**Ans.** There is no single flag or command to enable IP Masquerading and it varies upon your needs too. For this example we're enabling Masquerading for eth1 interface:

*user@server:/# modprobe ipt_MASQUERADE # Don't bother about any errors*

*user@server:/# iptables -F; iptables -t nat -F*

*user@server:/# iptables -t mangle -F*

*user@server:/# iptables -t nat -A POSTROUTING -o eth1 -j SNAT --to 10.0.0.1*

*user@server:/# echo 1 > /proc/sys/net/ipv4/ip_forward*

## Q51. As a Linux administrator which shell would you assign to a POP3 account?

**Ans.** Due to security reasons POP3 mail accounts are only assigned **/bin/false** or **/bin/nologin** shell account. If we don't do that then illegal usage of POP3 accounts can be conducted to download private email messages.

## Q52. How do you clear Swap memory cache?

**Ans.** Among other methods, following is the easiest one to follow. It just takes two commands and your swap will be free:

*user@server:/ #  swapoff −a*

*user@server:/ #  swapon -a*

## Q53. Where are the Samba log files stored?

**Ans.** Samba log files can be found in the traditional log folder such as **/varlog/samba/** or you can modify the config file (**smb.conf**) of samba to save it to a different location:

*[global]*

   *log file = / some-directory/ samba.%om.log*

## Q54. What are the basic commands for day to day user management?

**Ans.** Following are some most used commands:

• useradd

• userdel

• passwd

• newuser

• chown

• chmod

• lsof

- change

- last etc.

## Q55. Is there any file name limit in Linux? If yes then how many characters are maximum allowed?

**Ans.** A filename under Linux environment can hold up to as many as 255 characters maximum.

## Q56. What commands are used to check memory and CPU stats?

**Ans.** We can use **free** to check free and used memory and **vmstat** shows detailed statistics of virtual memory including process, paging, memory, block I/O, and traps.

## Q57. What is the purpose of Kali Linux?

**Ans.** Previously known as 'Backtrack', Kali Linux is one of the flavors of Linux based on Debian Linux. Its sole purpose is to help security specialists with compile and ready-to-use software packages to perform digital forensics and penetration testing to ensure optimum level of efficiency for the system or entire network.

## Q58. What is the purpose of *syslogd*?

**Ans. syslogd** is a demon which is responsible for tracking system information and saves them to appropriate log files.

## Q59. How do you change or remove the password assigned to a group?

**Ans**. We use gpasswd to change the password while gpassword with -r flag to remove the password.

## Q60. How do you setup a new cron job the easy way?

**Ans**. The easiest way to setup a cronjob is by running the **crontab** program with **-e** flag.

## Q61. How do you enter multiple commands in in one Go?

**Ans.** After typing each command we have to type in; semi-colon. Just like in some development languages a semi-colin is a line breaker, like-wise in Linux the semi-colon would tell the shell that a new command/line should be considered.

*user@server:/# ifconfig; iptables; ping 127.0.0.1 -c 3; vi*

## Q62. How would you define INODE?

**Ans.** INODE is a structure which is programmed to maintain information (such as file size, modification time, access, permission, etc.) and pointers to the data block of files that are stored in it.

## Q63. How do you check what messages appeared during the system boot?

**Ans. dmesg** command is used to check for what messaged were sent by system when it was booting. The command can be used in the following example:

*user@server:/# dmesg [option]*

## Q64. If you want to search for a particular term (i.e. "Salvador") in all the files existing under a specified directory and its subdirectories recursively, then what command would you enter?

**Ans.** we will use **grep** command with a separator to instruct result should be displayed line by line. Let's practice and observe:

*user@server:/# grep -woriI Salvador . | wc -l*

In the example above; the "." after Salvador represents the path to where to scan for and its sub directories. In this example "." Means current path, but it can be anything such as */var/log/* and the "**r**" flag tells the grep to look recursively while "**I**" flag ensures that matches in binary files are ignored. We can use "**w**" when we are searching for exact term and we can remove it if we want to search for something that could be something like "Salvador's". Nonetheless, if we want our search to be case-sensitive then we can add "**i**" switch to the above example next to **grep**. And in the end if we want to count how many times the occurrence of "Salvador" found in the files we can use "**wc −l**" after the vertical bar. Please note that we can remove any of the explained option/flag from our command if it's not required in the output result.

## Q65. Can you define private, unbindable, slave and shred mount points?

**Ans.** A **private mount** point is a mount point which is never shown elsewhere other than it's original location and it is not replicated unless they are explicitly mounted in other locations as well.

An **unbindable mount** point is a mount point which cannot be replicated anywhere under any circumstance

A **shared mount** is a mount point which can be replicated multiple times as needed and each replicated copy will continue to be exactly the same as the previous one.

A **slave mount point** is a mount point which is similar to shared mount point but it only receive mount and unmount events in a one way direction mode. That is to say, anything replicated to this mount point will not affect whatever will be mounted under this mount point.

## Q66. What is meant by terminal multiplexers? What are their purpose?

**Ans.** A terminal multiplexer will be a program which will allow the Linux shell to multiply terminals to be controlled through a single screen or through single remote session. Such programs help when you are logged in as a remote user but want to log off while keeping the program in running condition (i.e. installation of some software which may take time). These can also be used to split the single terminal in to two screen so we can conduct multiple actions at a same time under one session. Example of such terminal multiplexer are '**screen**' and '**tmux**'

## Q67. How to monitor any human readable log file in real-time using day to day handy Linux tool?

**Ans.** With the usage of **tail** command we can view any human readable log file in real time. By using additional flags and options we can achieve more or less depending on our need. Let's practice and observe:

*user@server:/# tail -F </path-to/log_file>*

This is a simple demonstration which will open the specified log file in real time but will then keep it open until it is terminated by the user manually. What additional options we can pass to this command is to set a time or a number of specific lines to be read in real time. For instance **-s** will specify for how many seconds the **tail** command should display the log file in real-time. **-n** option will tell the tail to display specific number of command and then terminate.

*user@server:/# tail -F -s 30 </path-to/log_file>*

*user@server:/# tail -n 50 -F </path-to/log_file>*

## Q68. What is a Linux Blackhole (or Linux null)? How it is different from a firewall packet filter and how do we add one?

**Ans.** A Blackhole is technically more of a generic networking technique than specifically a Linux command. It means to drop an IP address or a range of IP Address from the routing table so anything matching to the blackhole entry will simply be discarded silently without any message or further inspection. While a packet filter of a firewall may pose a similar option but it is different in the sense that firewall tend to inspect and most of the time send a specific reply to the prober, while a blackhole entry will simply be very silent and undetectable (unless and otherwise a manual thorough network investigation with deep analysis is conducted). We can add a blackhole in linux by typing the following commands:

*user@server:/# ip route add blackhole 10.0.0.1/32*

Above example will put 10.0.0.1 in to the blackhole

*user@server:/# ip route add blackhole 10.0.0.1/8*

This will put all the 10.0.0.1 – 10.255.255.254 rang in to blackhole.

## Q69. What Linux run level mode would you enter if you want to run the system in multi-user mode with networking?

**Ans.** Run level 3 serves the purpose of running the system in multi-user mode with networking support. These level can be triggered from within the running session of Linux console or can be configured manually/permanently to take affect during the boot time.

## Q70. What is the purpose of strace command?

**Ans**. Main usage of **strace** command is to check system called by a program. Thus, the purpose of **strace** is being useful against debugging and benchmarking.

## Q71. If you want to stop a running script which command will put the script to sleep mode until further signal is received?

**Ans. suspend** command will put any script to sleep until further signals are received.

## Q72. What are the functions of 'hash' command?

**Ans. hash** command can perform the following functions:

• To manage internal hash table

• To trace and remember the full path of the command being specified

• To display the names of command used and the number of hits

## Q73. What is the purpose of bind command in a Linux shell?

**Ans.** The purpose of bind command in Linux shell are:

• To define new macros

• To define newly binded keys for existing commands

• To define dumping of the installed key bindings

## Q74. Does '*time*' command show current date and time?

**Ans.** No, many newbies of Linux type in **time** command to check the current date and time. The correct command to check and configure current date and time is '**date**'.

## Q75. What would you do if you want to display content of a file but one page at a time?

**Ans.** we can use cat command to achieve this task followed by more with vertical bar. Example:

*user@server:/# cat /home/fred/readme.txt | more*

## Q76. What is the purpose of stty command?

**Ans. stty** command is used to set the IO characteristic of terminal

## Q77. What directory does the ~ symbol represents?

**Ans.** In the path, or when accessing through Shell, the ~ symbol will always refer to the home directory of currently logged in user.

## Q78. What mode will make the file executable?

**Ans.** In order to make your file/script executable type in the following command

*user@server:/# chmod +x filename.sh*


## Q79. What is the command to rename a file or folder in Linux?

**Ans.** Many newbies who migrate from Windows to Linux wonder about the alternate of '**ren**' or '**rename**' command in Linux. But in reality there is no exact alternate, rather we have to use 'mv command to perform the function. Example:

*user@server:/# mv oldfilename newfilename*

Make sure the **newfilename** does not already exist, otherwise mv command will overwrite without prompting


## Q80. What is the UID number of user root?

**Ans.** UID number of user root will always be 0


## Q81. Does *pwd* command change the password for username?

**Ans.** As a newbie some may confused this command for that purpose, but actually this command only tells the current working path of the logged in user.

## Q82. Please describe the functions of sysfs?

**Ans.** sysfs command performs the folowing:

• serves the purpose as a virtual file system

• gives information about the running kernel to currently logged in users

• help in exporting kernel objects

## Q83. What is the pid number of init process?

**Ans.** the PID number for init process is 1 because it is one of the first program to run when Linux boots.

## Q84. What is the last **PID** number that could exist in Linux?

**Ans.** Although Linux is a very big Operating system and very flexible but it has a default limit PID 32768.

## Q85. What is the function of Buffer Cache?

**Ans.** Buffer Cache keeps a pool of internal data buffer by letting the kernel minimize the frequency of disk access and to increase the response time and throughput.

## Q86. Why it is wise to login as a user account instead of root?

**Ans.** If you are migrating from Windows to Linux, or if you are a regular windows user but you have some work/project on Linux; you might want to boot your Linux and login as root account assuming that it is equivalent of windows' administrator account. Although it indeed is pretty much the same thing but with Linux infrastructure, it is believed that logging in from root account can open the windows for attackers to gain unauthorized access to your system. It can also lead a malicious program to gain access of your system, or if a program is malfunctioning it will have all the read/write/execute. Therefor to minimize the damage and to be on safe side, it is advised not to login as root.

For the same purpose, Debian and any other distro based on Debian uses the **'sudo'** command which lets you run programs which require root privileges but doesn't log you in as root user. Remember that not all programs require root access and thus **sudo** is only used with selected programs only.

## Q87. What should be an ideal swap partition size for your Linux box?

**Ans.** The idea size of a swap partition should be double the size of RAM (physical memory) installed on your system. If the disk space or other restrictions won't let you do this, then the minimum preferred swap partition size is at least the same size of your system's physical memory.

## Q88. What are symbolic links in Linux file system?

**Ans.** Symbolic links are similar to the 'shortcut' feature in Windows. The purpose of symlinks it to provide you direct access to the specified file or directory without the need of typing out the full path (usually if it is long one) location of it.

## Q89. How would you refer the physical parallel ports under a Linux file system?

**Ans.** While with windows parallel ports are referred as LPT1 LPT2 LPT3 and so on, under a Linux system they are simply located at */dev/* with label lp0 lp1 lp2 lp3 and so on.

## Q90. Name main and most popular Linux distributions from which various other distros are derived.

**Ans.** Mainly there are 2 big and major distribution; Redhat or CentOS and Debian, from which many other distributions are derived (even Kali Linux is based on debian). However distros like Gentoo, slackware and OpenSuse also have some influence on other distros which are derived from them.

## Q91. Name any top 5 major Linux distribution of all time?

**Ans.** Redhat, CentOS, Debian, OpenSuse, Gentoo

## Q92. What is a */dev/ttyS0* in a Linux system?

**Ans.** */dev/ttyS0* simply refers to the very first serial port of your computer in the series. That is to say, the more serial ports your computer has the longer number of ttyS series will be (from S0 to S7). For example:

*/dev/ttyS0*

*/dev/ttyS1*

*/dev/ttyS2*

...

*/dev/ttyS7*

**Please note** that these serial ports are same as what you refer as COM1 - COM8 under a windows system.

# Chapter 3:
# Job responsibilities of Linux admin and how to execute it

Depending on the company's needs and requirement may vary. Generally following responsibilities are common for a Linux administrator on day to day basis:

**Efficient with Internet Applications**: Hands-on experience required on applications like DNS, Apache, RADIUS, MySQL, PHP. Anything which is required by the company; for instance it could be nginx instead of Apache and Squid instead of any other common proxying program. MariaDB for MySQL and JAVA/HTML instead of PHP. Although PHP/HTML and JAVA falls in to web administration level of expertise but it is highly preferred if one is well equipped with at least these three programs.

**Backup and Disaster Recovery**: Taking frequent backup OR make an automated scheduled backup of server(s). Must know how to recover data in crises moments such as disaster recovery. Must know how to secure data and keep backup in location(s) that are secure and well recoverable once data restoration is required. Must know how to use the most of the following programs for backup and restoration purses. Rsync,Fwbackup, Bacula, backupninja, sbackup, etc.

**Supervision:** If you're hired as a senior Linux admin, you should be able to train and support other server admins who comes under your supervision.

**Troubleshoot & Customer Support:** Review all of the error logs (on daily basis) while reviewing other normal logs too in case of requirement. Fixing the errors found in the logs and customer support (troubleshooting the queries asked by clients) if this is also part of your company.

**Communications Skill:** Although some admins do not interact with customers that often, but a really good admin should be courteous and professional when communicating with the customers, vendors and the staff itself.

**Management:** It's responsibility of every Linux administrator to install the necessary procedures and security applications. He will be responsible for working with Data Network Engineers and other concerned personnel in order to conduct analysis on hardware requirements and suggest for acquisition recommendations.

**Upgrading software:** This goes parallel to backup and restoration responsibility. Every admin is responsible for upgrading the installed software or apply patches for whichever software is available on internet as quickly as they are updated on internet. Upgradation may vary from upgrading webserver applications, firewall tools, frameworks, etc.

**Familiar with Applications:** You are responsible to be friendly with all the concerned application installed on the Linux system, to extend that if there are issues arises you must know to troubleshoot the server.

**Monitoring:** Monitoring the services most probably in real-time is also part of important duties of a Linux administration, especially if you are hired for a large scale company. Nowadays not everything is monitored manually and we can always view logs and have trigger systems - but there are certain scenarios and circumstances when manual monitor becomes mandatory (such as when server or network is under a live attack etc.).

**Maintenance:** Conducting daily performance tuning of the system, upgradation of hardware whenever necessary, optimization of resources as and when required. Configuration of disk partition and file management look after as and when required.

**Security:** Your Company may have a different personnel for security of the network, but it is ALWAYS handy and very beneficial if you are yourself skilled with securing the system and the network connected to and from your system. Master the art of packet filtering, iptables, pfsense, fail2ban and learn how does netstat and running process correlate to each other in terms of detecting an attack or malware on the system.

# Chapter 4:
# Troubleshooting Q&A or scenarios

**Q. How would you differentiate between IP-based virtual hosting and name-based virtual hosting? Can you explain in a scenario where name-based virtual hosting can be fit useful?**

**Ans.** IP based virtual host can run multiple web site from one server machine but each of the website will have its own IP Address in contrast to name based host where all the website will have same ip address.

Virtual host based hosting consist of multiple domains under one single IP address. The workaround is to have all the domains linked to single IP address either identified uniquely by different port number within one instance of apache or more appropriately, different path using single different domains under single IP. For example:

*www.fred.com --> /home/fred/public_html/*

*www.alice.com --> /home/alice/public_html/*

*www.joe.com --> /home/joe/public_html/*

In a scenario where shared webhosting is being offered to the customers, it will be very costly to assign a dedicated IP address to all the customers. Best solution will be to follow the name based virtual hosting so that each user is assigned a different path on the server instead of whole new IP Address.

## Q. What would you do in case of a failed installation?

**Ans.** Conducting the verification of the data by performing a checksum to the downloaded installation image/disc should be the very initial step to be taken when such issue arise. In any case if the checksum fails, you can re-burn the disc or re-download the image (preferably from a different location than you previously tried - in case if your internet wasn't the fault behind the corrupt image downloaded image).

## Q. What to do when facing the slow and slugging performance?

**Ans.** Performance based issues are either caused by Hardware or a troubled process. First thing to make sure is checking the trouble process (since hardware issues are not frequent compared to process based issues). Process monitoring tools such as 'top' command should be able to give you good details about the running processes and should be able to help you determine if the performance issue is process based. If it is indeed process based, then checking the logs for the culprit process should reveal why it is taking more than usual memory, it could be a faulty code, script or even a cyber-attack. A detail investigation probe may be required in some cases.

Since performance is quite closely related to RAM in the case of hardware issue; RAM should be the very first component to diagnose for being damaged or corrupt. If you're using desktop then the graphics card can be considered too. There are some tools which can help detect faulty RAM from Linux shell, such as memtest86+, memtester, etc.

## Q. How do you solve GRUB related issues?

**Ans**. Most of the GRUB related issues are caused by misconfigured config file or corrupt/deleted partition. In order to combat such issues, your primary tool should be GRUB utility (installed and booted from an external media). Plan B can be booting up your system using the LiveCD of the same distro (preferably) then if its partition issue; open up the GParted tool to fix the issue, else correct the misconfigured GRUB if it's the configuration issue.

## Q. What are Kernel Panic issues and how do you troubleshoot them?

**Ans.** Most Kernel Panics are caused by unhandled processor exceptions within the kernel code itself. Defective or incompatible RAM are one of the most leading causes of kernel Panics.

Kernel panics are very difficult to identify and troubleshoot at most of the times. Troubleshooting a kernel panic will usually require reproducing a situation that may not occur quite often and then collect the data that is quite difficult to gather

Depending on the nature of a kernel panic, Kernel itself will probably log all the useful information about the crash/panic just before going in to lock up mode. Following are the important pieces of information we should gather up. Not all of the following information may be available (since kernel panic could be a very devastating crash) so there for collecting as many information as many possible is the key goal here.

• */var/log/messages* (if you are lucky then entire kernel panic stack could have been posted here by kernel and ultimately it will make troubleshooting lot less difficult)

• Application or Library logs (cheetah, RTF, etc.) should be able to show what was happening prior to kernel panic

• Copy the error messages shown on the screen. (You can copy them by manually writing them on your notebook or taking a picture from your cell phone)

## Q. Installed Linux for the first time and you get kernel panic error. What would you do?

**Ans.** Usually the kernel panic error you see right after installing the Linux is not a major crash issue. Following steps can be taken to resolve this issue:

• Go to GRUB (which is the very first thing which will come up prior to loading the Linux).

• In order for the GRUB to load the Linux, it should know where the Linux Kernel is located. It location is saved in the GRUB config file located at */boot/grub/grub.conf* file. If you have incorrectly set the location for the Linux Kernel it will cause kernel panic error.

• Properly configure the GRUB config file and point the root filesystem and kernel correctly.

## Q. If one of the application starts creating humongous large sized core dump files, what would you do as an administrator if you don't have any intention to debug those files?

**Ans.** If you don't have any intentions of keeping those dump files for debugging purposes, then you should delete them because they are taking up plenty of valuable space and may eventually cause the system to run out of space too.

**Q. If for some reasons you need to terminate the sendmail process what would you do?**

**Ans.** There are two ways to achieve this, first one is to figure out the PID of **sendmail** and then kill that pid. The other one is to run **killall** command with **sendmail** process name. For example:

*user@server:/# ps -ef |grep sendmail*

*user@server:/# kill <pid#>*

Or

*user@server:/# killall grep sendmail*

**Q. If you notice a kernel error message during the Linux boot process, but all of a sudden that error is scrolled up before you could possibly read it, which of the log files would you check to see that message you missed?**

**Ans.** All the boot messages are stored in ***/var/log/dmesg*** file. So if the kernel has given error message during the boot process it should also be available in that same file.

# Chapter 5:
# Tips on how to prepare for interview

Preparing for an interview for the post of Linux administrator can be as generic as preparing for any other technical job. However there can be few things which can be considered such as:

• Seek the background information of the job requirement. For instance, things which were mentioned in the Job ad; you should be able to thoroughly answer anything concerned to skills or requirements mentioned

• Take some free online tests about question and answers regard Linux. You should be able to score at least 85% on all the tests you are taking, in order to assume yourself eligible to give the interview

• Memorizing all the important questions. Be prepared for tricky scenarios that may have very easy solutions

• Memorize all the important questions

• Be punctual

• Be prepared for tricky scenarios that may have very solutions

• Paying attention is the key, tricky scenarios with easy solutions are easily detected if you are paying enough detailed attention to what is being asked

• Prepare yourself for any possible practical exam. They may give you a live system in front of you and give you task. It may not be very difficult but they are usually day to day tasks they'd want to test you for

• Your Team leading qualities may be tested if you are applying for a senior administrator job

• Dress appropriately, all though Linux geeks may want to pose a fancy l33t guy impression but generally companies STILL look for professional looking administrators. So keep the fancy geek attitude inside of you and bring out the professional appearance instead

• When asked about "yourself", do not start bragging about your achievements which are not relevant to company's benefit. Keep it tight to your concerned academic achievements, any projects you have completed and brief history of your education.

• Switch off your cell phone before entering the room. You may probably want to an impression that you're a very busy and in-demand person; but it doesn't work most of the time and it is considered impolite

# Chapter 6:
# Conclusion

Full administration requires an in-depth knowledge of different components of system. Linux maybe an experience of jumping in to the ocean. Sometimes you'd feel like drowning, but there are many helping resources out there to get you equipped with knowledge so that you could swim in smoothly and learn as much as possible.

As far as interviews are concerned, judging your confidence and personality is equally important as much as your knowledge is. There may be a high chance that you are not confident but you can still be a really good geek with Linux, but many times a company is seeking for a confident Team leader or a person who could convince and communicate well within the company and to the customers.

*As an author I highly appreciate the feedback I get from my readers. It helps others to make an informed decision before buying my book. If You have enjoyed this book please consider leaving a short review at the following link.*

*Please visit https://www.amazon.com/review/create-review?asin=B0793LSXXS to write a review.*

# Recommended Books:

Linux Administrator Top Interview Question and Answers By Mark Tim

Linux Security Beyond System Administration By Mark Tim

Network Admin Top Interview Questions and Answers By Mark Tim

Interview Question And Answers For AWS Developers And Architects By Mark Tim

Azure Top Interview Questions and Answers By Mark Tim

Day to Day tasks and solutions of Network Administrators By Mike Ryan

AWS Top Interview Questions and Answers By Mike Ryan

VMware Administrator Interview Question And Answers By Brian Williams